AR PTS: 0.5

Brands We Know

McDonald's

By Sara Green

Bellwether Media • Minneapolis, MN

Jump into the cockpit and take flight with Pilot books. Your journey will take you on high-energy adventures as you learn about all that is wild, weird, fascinating, and fun!

This edition first published in 2015 by Bellwether Media, Inc.

No part of this publication may be reproduced in whole or in part without written permission of the publisher.
For information regarding permission, write to Bellwether Media, Inc.,
Attention: Permissions Department,
5357 Penn Avenue South, Minneapolis, MN 55419.

Library of Congress Cataloging-in-Publication Data

Green, Sara, 1964-
 McDonald's / by Sara Green.
    pages cm. -- (Pilot: Brands We Know)
 Includes bibliographical references and index.
 Summary: "Engaging images accompany information about the
McDonald's Corporation. The combination of high-interest subject
matter and narrative text is intended for students in grades 3 through
7"-- Provided by publisher.
 Audience: 7-12.
 Audience: Grades 3-7.
 ISBN 978-1-62617-209-8 (hardcover : alk. paper)
1. McDonald's Corporation--Juvenile literature. 2. Fast food
restaurants--United States--Juvenile literature. I. Title.
 TX945.5.M33G74 2015
 647.9573--dc23
                          2014034773

Table of Contents

What Is McDonald's?

Sometimes people do not have time to cook. For them, a quick meal may be a short drive away. They look for McDonald's Golden Arches. Soon their grumbling bellies will be full!

McDonald's is the largest fast-food hamburger **chain** on Earth. It serves inexpensive sandwiches, salads, and drinks. Many people also enjoy its french fries, shakes, and breakfast foods. Low prices, tasty food, and top customer service have helped the chain achieve great success. In 2014, McDonald's was worth more than $96 billion! It is also one of the world's most well-known **brands**. People all over the globe recognize the famous Golden Arches as the **symbol** for the restaurant chain.

By the Numbers

119
countries with a
McDonald's restaurant

$77 million
in sales each day

more than
500 million
Big Macs sold per year

more than
35,000
restaurants around
the world

about
9 million
pounds (4 million kilograms)
of french fries served
each day

1.9 million
employees

The McDonald Brothers

McDonald's has not always been known for its hamburgers. In 1940, brothers Richard and Maurice McDonald opened a drive-in restaurant in San Bernardino, California. They called it "McDonald's Famous Barbecue." Its menu was large and **carhops** served the food to customers. The restaurant was successful, but the brothers wanted to do better. Around that time, the number of highways began to increase. More people drove to restaurants. The brothers realized that these traveling customers were looking for inexpensive food and speedy service.

San Bernardino,
California

Let's eat out!
1960s tagline

LICENSEE OF **McDonald's**
SPEEDEE SERVICE SYSTEM
HAMBURGERS
We have Sold OVER 1 MILLION

In 1948, the brothers changed their restaurant. They shortened the name to "McDonald's." Their new menu had only nine items. Customers ordered food at restaurant windows and ate it in their cars. The brothers prepared orders using an **assembly line** system. Food arrived shortly after a customer placed an order. Customers loved the new menu and fast service. Soon, the brothers opened more restaurants. They added a pair of golden arches to each new building. The symbol attracted drivers and pulled in more customers.

Ray Kroc

In 1954, McDonald's caught the attention of a salesman named Ray Kroc. Ray sold milk shake mixers to restaurants. The McDonald brothers were among his top customers. Ray wanted to see how they sold so many milk shakes. He traveled to San Bernardino and parked his car outside the restaurant. Lines of people were waiting to buy food. Ray realized the brothers had created something special. This sparked an idea. Why not open more McDonald's across the country?

Ray urged the brothers to open more restaurants. They did not want this responsibility, but they liked Ray's enthusiasm. The brothers sold Ray the **rights** to open McDonald's **franchises**. On April 15, 1955, Ray opened his first McDonald's in Des Plaines, Illinois. His business **motto** was "Quality, Service, Cleanliness, and Value." Soon, Ray built more restaurants. In 1959, the 100th McDonald's opened in Fond du Lac, Wisconsin.

Ray Kroc

Look for the Golden Arches

1960s tagline

May I Take Your Order?

The first McDonald's drive-thru opened in 1975 in Arizona. It was created to serve soldiers from a nearby military base. They were not allowed out of their cars in uniform.

Did somebody say McDonald's?

1990s-2000s tagline

Ray was thrilled about the chain's success. However, he had even bigger dreams for McDonald's. He wanted to open thousands more restaurants. Richard and Maurice did not share these dreams. So in 1961, Ray bought the rights to the McDonald's name from the brothers for $2.7 million. Ray then put his own ideas in place. He wanted all McDonald's restaurants to have the same look, menu, and prices. He also wanted food preparation and service to be standard. In 1961, Ray opened a training center in Illinois called Hamburger University. There, managers learned how to operate a McDonald's according to Ray's wishes.

Ray's company was prospering. Then, in 1963, a new character helped McDonald's become even more famous. A cheerful clown named Ronald McDonald appeared in a television commercial for the first time. Later, Hamburglar, Grimace, and other characters joined Ronald in McDonaldland. These beloved characters gave McDonald's a huge popularity boost. Now they are recognized around the world!

Ronald McDonald

Menus Around the World

The McDonald's menu has grown since 1948. Today, customers can choose from more than 100 items! A franchise owner in Pennsylvania invented one of the most popular foods. In 1967, Jim Delligatti made a two-patty hamburger called the Big Mac. It was an instant hit with customers. Millions of Big Macs are still sold every day.

Jim Delligatti

Big Mac

Chicken McNugget Happy Meal

Egg McMuffin

Shamrock Shake

Happy Meals were introduced for children in 1979. They had a circus theme and came with a hamburger or cheeseburger. They also included fries, cookies, a soft drink, and a toy. Today, kids have more choices. Chicken McNuggets are a popular option. Apples and milk are other new additions.

Other favorite menu items include the Filet-O-Fish sandwich, the Egg McMuffin, and the McDouble. The Shamrock Shake is also popular. This green dessert was invented in 1970. It is only sold in February and March in honor of St. Patrick's Day. Every year, people look forward to drinking this minty treat.

McDonald's has fans all over the world. The first **international** McDonald's restaurants opened in Canada and Puerto Rico in 1967. Today, McDonald's restaurants are found in more than 100 countries. Antarctica is the only continent that does not have a McDonald's!

International menus have many of the same items found on American menus. Customers can usually find french fries, shakes, and other popular foods. However, McDonald's menus vary from country to country. Different cultures have their own food preferences. For example, customers can order pies filled with red bean paste in Japan. **Vegetarian** burgers are on the menu in India, where many people do not eat meat. In the Philippines, McSpaghetti is a top seller. Even in the United States, the menu has a few **regional** differences. McLobster rolls are often on the menu in Maine. In Hawaii, customers can order Spam, Eggs, and Rice.

McDonald's Around the World

Country	Food
Brazil	Cheese Quiche
China	Mashed Potato Beef Burger
India	McAloo Tikki (spiced potato patty)
Japan	Ebi Filet-O (shrimp burger)
Malaysia	Bubur Ayam McD (chicken porridge)
Nicaragua	Mango Pie
The Philippines	McSpaghetti
Spain	Gazpacho (cold vegetable soup)
Switzerland	Macaroons
United Kingdom	Fish Fingers

Macaroons
(Switzerland)

McAloo Tikki
(India)

Fish Fingers
(United Kingdom)

ماكدونالدز

An International Sensation

In 1994, the first McDonald's opened in Kuwait, a country in the Middle East. On the day it opened, many customers waited in a drive-thru line for food. The line reached 7 miles (11.3 kilometers) long!

Changes for the Better

McDonald's has been very successful. However, the company realizes that people's preferences change. It must **adapt** in order to keep its customers happy. The McDonald's menu has many foods that are high in fat and salt. These unhealthy foods have been keeping more and more customers away. In response, the chain has already begun adding healthier food choices. Customers can find more fruits, vegetables, and **whole grains** on the menu. These are more **nutritious** than burgers and fries.

McDonald's is also making changes to protect the environment. Today, many McDonald's restaurants use **LED** lighting to save energy. The company also wants to cut all in-restaurant waste in half by 2020. The source of food items is also changing. McDonald's gets some eggs from **cage-free** chickens. Soon, beef will come from farmers who raise cattle in a way that reduces **emissions**. The company is also working to get coffee, cooking oil, and other **imports** only from **sustainable** sources. Through these efforts, McDonald's is making a difference.

Ronald McDonald House Charities

McDonald's also helps people. The McDonald's Corporation supports an organization called the Ronald McDonald House **Charities**. This organization helps improve children's health and well-being. One way it does this is through Ronald McDonald Houses. These houses are located all over the world. Sometimes, children need to be treated in hospitals far from home. Ronald McDonald Houses give family members a free or inexpensive place to stay near hospitals. Parents can stay close to their children to help them get well.

Ronald McDonald House Charities also supports Ronald McDonald Care Mobiles. These large vehicles travel to poor communities in the United States and other countries. Medical professionals give children check-ups and **vaccinations**. They teach families about health care and nutrition. The Care Mobiles also provide dental care to children. Dentists treat tooth **decay** and other painful conditions. They teach children how to keep their teeth clean. Ronald McDonald House Charities has helped thousands of children around the world stay healthy. It is just one way McDonald's gives back to its communities.

i'm lovin' it
2000s-2010s tagline

19

McDonald's Timeline

1940
Richard and Maurice McDonald open McDonald's Famous Barbecue in San Bernardino, California

1961
Hamburger University opens in Elk Grove Village, Illinois

1954
Ray Kroc first visits McDonald's in San Bernardino, California

1963
Ronald McDonald appears in his first television commercial

1979
Happy Meals are introduced

1968
The Big Mac appears on menus nationwide

1955
Ray Kroc opens his first McDonald's in Des Plaines, Illinois

1967
The first international McDonald's restaurants open in Canada and Puerto Rico

1948
Richard and Maurice reopen McDonald's as a self-service restaurant

1962
A McDonald's in Denver, Colorado, becomes the first to have indoor seating

1974
The first Ronald McDonald House opens in Philadelphia, Pennsylvania

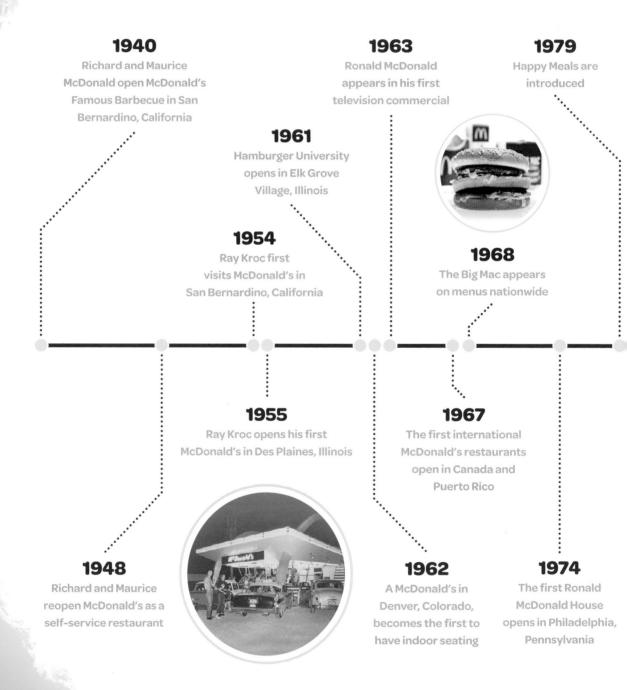

1988

Fortune magazine names
McDonald's hamburgers
as one of the top 100 items
America makes best

2004

Happy Meals begin offering
healthier choices such as
apples and milk

2002

The Dollar Menu
is created

2011

McDonald's has restaurants
in 119 countries

1984

Ray Kroc
passes away

Countries with McDonald's = ■

Glossary

adapt—to adjust to changes

assembly line—an arrangement of workers or machines where work passes from one to the next until a product is put together

brands—categories of products all made by the same company

cage-free—not raised in a cage; cage-free chickens can roam around a barn.

carhops—food servers at drive-in restaurants

chain—a set of related restaurants or businesses with the same name

charities—organizations that help others in need

decay—rotting

emissions—dangerous fumes

franchises—restaurants or businesses operated by people only after they received permission from the companies that own the rights to the restaurants or businesses

imports—products from other countries

international—outside of the United States

LED—a form of light that saves energy; LED stands for light-emitting diode.

motto—a short sentence or phrase that expresses what someone believes

nutritious—healthy

regional—special for a certain area

rights—the legal ability to use a certain name or product

sustainable—able to be used without being completely used up or destroyed

symbol—a thing that stands for something else

vaccinations—injections that help prevent diseases

vegetarian—made without meat

whole grains—grains that have not been processed; whole grains have more nutrients than processed grains.

To Learn More

AT THE LIBRARY

Gilbert, Sara. *The Story of McDonald's*. Mankato, Minn.: Creative Education, 2009.

Schrier, Allyson Valentine. *Eat Right: Your Guide to Maintaining a Healthy Diet*. Mankato, Minn.: Capstone Press, 2012.

Watson, Stephanie. *Fast Food*. New York, N.Y.: The Rosen Pub. Group, 2008.

ON THE WEB

Learning more about McDonald's is as easy as 1, 2, 3.

1. Go to www.factsurfer.com.

2. Enter "McDonald's" into the search box.

3. Click the "Surf" button and you will see a list of related web sites.

With factsurfer.com, finding more information is just a click away.

Index

The images in this book are reproduced through the courtesy of: McDonald's Corporation, front cover (cheeseburger), table of contents, pp. 4 (top, bottom), 12 (top), 13 (top, center, bottom), 15 (top, top bottom), 16; saknakom, p. 5; Brian Cahn/ Corbis, p. 7; Art Shay/ Getty Images, p. 8; Brian Cahn/ ZUMA Press/ Corbis, p. 9; Mark Blinch/ Reuters/ Corbis, p. 10; Settawat Udom, p. 11; Sean Stipp/ AP Images, p. 12 (bottom); Guang Niu/ Staff/ Getty Images, p. 14; Associated Press/ AP Images, p. 15 (top center); Paul Doyle/ Getty Images, p. 15 (bottom); Tooykrub, p. 17; Peter Kramer/ Staff/ Getty Images, p. 19; Everett Collection/ Newscom, p. 20 (left); spflaum1, p. 20 (right); McDonald's Corporation/ ABDESIGN, p. 21 (top).